BLUFFER'S
TO
BLUFFING

PETER GAMMOND

with a Conthology by
ALAN HANKINSON

ЯR

RAVETTE BOOKS

Published by Ravette Books Limited
Egmont House
25/31 Tavistock Place
London WC1H 9SU
(071) 344 6400

First printed 1987
Reprinted 1991, 1992, 1994

Series Editor – Anne Tauté

Cover design – Jim Wire
Printing & Binding – Cox & Wyman Ltd.
Production – Oval Projects Ltd.

The Bluffer's Guides® is a
Registered Trademark.

The Bluffer's Guides® series is based
on an original idea by Peter Wolfe.

An Oval Project
for Ravette Books Ltd.

CONTENTS

The Bluffer's Mantra

When tact and truth are not enough
The honest man must turn to bluff.

INTRODUCTION

The Bluffer's Guides were thought up one Sunday afternoon, some 20 years ago, by the now legendary Peter Wolfe. Enjoying great success and prestige under his fatherly guidance, the saga only came to a temporary halt when Peter Wolfe decided to become a serious publisher.

In response to public demand, this important series has now been revived and continued by a sideways looking organisation that prefers to remain nameless. And who can blame it? Originally the Bluffer's Guides extended to a dozen or so titles. It is now intended to expand the series to some 3,667 titles, thus providing a volume on virtually every subject that a bluffer could wish to bluff in – and some they would not.

The whole principle and philosophy of the Guides was neatly summed up by Peter Clayton, then a perceptive columnist of the *Sunday Telegraph*, who said:

> The Bluffer's Guides have been written on the principle that a little learning is a marvellous thing, and since that is all most of us are ever going to have anyway, we might as well get to know how to spread it thinly, but effectively, like the yeast extract you put on bread.'

The proprietors, directors, editors, artists, charladies and close relatives living at the Bluffer's Guides palatial headquarters, together with the printers, typesetters, and binders are unanimous in their desire to accept no final responsibility for anything to be found in these volumes. Only the authors (they say) are to blame, which doesn't seem fair as they get so little out of it. But who has ever been fair to authors, and why should they be expected to start now?

While we must warmly express our gratitude to anyone who has bought or borrowed one of these Guides, we cannot accept any blame for any lowering of living or moral standards that have resulted from such purchase or appropriation.

> WARNING: The contents of this book are dangerous and could cause permanent damage to the brain. It should be read only by genuine bluffers. Medium-to-high blah.

DEFINITION OF BLUFFING

bluff, *v* 1674. (of unknown etym. Prob. a cant Restoration term. Recent users seem to connect with BLUFF *a*. or *sb*. (ie. big, surly, blustering) and make it mean 'to hoodwink by assuming a fictitious bold front') 1. *trans* To blindfold or hoodwink. 2. In the game of poker: To impose upon (an opponent) as to the strength of one's hand, by betting heavily upon it, or the like, so as to induce him to throw up the game. (Of U.S. origin.) Hence *transf*: 1864. 3. *intr*. To attempt the imposition described in 2. 1882. Hence **Bluffer**.

> Taken, with acknowledgement, from
> *The Shorter Oxford English Dictionary*

bluff. A considerable assurance adopted to impress an opponent: orig (1848) U.S. anglicized ca 1870: cf. the v. Coll. 2. In low s., an excuse: a sense firmly grounded in England – see Mayhew's *London Labour* – as early as 1851: this sense may, perhaps, not come from the U.S.

bluffer. In c. of mid-C.17-early 19, 'a Host, Inn Keeper or Victualler', B.E.; Coles, 1676. Prob. ex dial. **bluff**, to hoodwink, 2. An imposer who relies on an assumed appearance and speech: from ca 1885; coll. 3. A bosun: nautical: ca 1840-1914.

bluffing. vbl n. 'Imposing on another with a show of force where no real force exists: a phrase taken from the game of poker', Thornton, who records it for U.S. at 1850. Anglicized, as coll, ca 1880.

> Taken, with acknowledgement, from
> *A Dictionary of Historical Slang* by Eric Partridge

The common poker usage is ideal for our purpose. We prefer not to use the term 'hoodwink', as a fine distinction must be drawn between the gentle art of bluffing and actually lying or cheating. The hood-winker is out to deceive, the bluffer merely wishes to keep another person in a state of uncertainty.

The true aim of civilised bluffing is to hold your own against (not actually to humble or defeat) a social, intellectual or business opponent. The bluffer does not intend to be outwitted by anyone, especially by someone who clearly has a superior fund of knowledge.

Victory is achieved if you can force your opponent to 'throw up' (cf. 1, sub-section 2, above) before you do. You may mentally score:

- three points for an away win, i.e. competing against a superior intellect

- two points for a draw, if against an equal

- one point if your opponent is clearly an idiot.

The latter is the commonest score.

In these days of widespread public bluffing, the simple bluff is often too mild. Life is easier if you can master such assets as the double-bluff, and the triple-bluff.

The **Double** (or Bi-bluff) is now commonly used. This involves speaking the truth as if it was a bluff, so that people think you are bluffing when you aren't.

The **Triple** (or Tri-bluff) is even more difficult to handle and should only be used by experts. Here the bluff is made in the normal way to sound like the truth, but the truth is itself a bluff. Much employed by politicians and churchmen.

THE GENTLE ART OF BLUFF

Why Bluffing is Necessary

Elizabethan man (c. 1650) was considered a well-rounded individual if he:

a) knew a little about all the arts
b) could use a sword, and
c) knew who the current monarch was.

It was much easier in olden times. There had not been anything like as much history as there has been since; and the maps were still half empty. Nor had science really got going, and nobody was expected to understand computers. The arts were all pretty basic and even royalty wrote music. A little learning was an ample thing.

The present day Elizabethan II man (c. now) has so much to know that the chances of being anything more than half-rounded are slight. Even those who know everything there is to know about their chosen subject (e.g. Sheridan Morley on theatre; David Bellamy on fungus; Melvyn Bragg on anything) may be found sadly wanting in other departments.

At the same time the means of getting to know about almost any topic are unfortunately reasonably accessible. Not to know is simply an admission of mental lassitude. The successful man or woman of today, especially those who read the Sunday magazines, likes to appear to be in touch with more or less everything. They may not be really interested in, say, comprehensive education, isomorphism or open-cast coal-mining, but they are expected to converse on any of these subjects at a moment's notice.

It is on these occasions that a careful manipulation of some basic facts will help them to bluff their way through with a reasonable degree of nonchalance. Failure to buff up one's bluffing techniques can only leave one in a continual state of chalance.

General Applications of Bluffing

Any suggestion that bluffing is merely the resort of the ignorant (however heavily they may depend on it) is to be dismissed. The learned professor is no less in need of its cushioning effect than anyone else. Indeed, judicial bluffing is essential here, to cover the gaps in what is supposed to be an infallible fund of knowledge.

In Music, for example, the general practitioner is constantly open to attack by the specialist – i.e. the kind who knows all about Gerald Finzi, Jeremiah Clarke, or Horsecollar Draper (see Jazz) and will only be budged with reluctance from that particular area. Here the knowledge of some diversionary facts (even fictitious facts in desperate cases) will come in handy. You must learn how to steer the conversation away from people's specialities and counter-attack with any of the other 3,566 subjects that they clearly know little about.

Favourite subjects for bluffing used to be Politics, Religion and Sex. But these are not anything like as popular as they once were. Indeed, they are even taboo as subjects of conversation in some areas of public life, e.g. Cabinet meetings or Rotary clubs.

A survey carried out by the John Courtis organisation reveals that the most talked-about subjects today are Money, Children, Education, Holidays (and the Money spent on them), Television, Food, Drink and Money.

The occasions when bluffing most comes in useful are:

a) as a means of self-defence; the 'assumption of a fictitious bold front' at parties and other tedious functions

b) in confrontation with shopkeepers. They will always try to convince you that what they have in stock is superior to the item that you came in to get and which they haven't got at the moment. Be ready with a good line of scientific twaddle that will leave them speechless

c) in certain trades or professions; where a degree of bluffing is essential to convince yourself and others that you know what you are talking about. Of particular importance to Lawyers, Salesmen, Estate Agents, Teachers, Printers and Plumbers

d) in business (see under Business)

e) all the time in everything. Bluffing is not simply a game to be played at parties but can be a whole way of life.

How to Recognise a Bluffer

The Practised or Accomplished male bluffer may be recognised by the bland composure of his features, and by the way his eyes focus on a point in the middle of your forehead. The female of the species is deadlier in most ways, and will often look you straight in the eye.

The Professional bluffer, e.g. the Politician, is not easy to tackle. They are so practised in every aspect of their art that it is always difficult to find a chink in their armour. When you are up against someone whose whole strategy is bluff, you may then, totally against your natural inclinations, have to resort to truth. So always have a truth or two in reserve; though this sort of thing certainly doesn't want to be overdone.

The Casual or Novice bluffer is easy to spot because he keeps looking at a small, inexpensive book in the palm of his hand. Don't let him see yours.

The Know-All and the Expert

It is inevitable if you are a regular bluffer that you will be drawn into discussions in which a Know-All is also involved. Here is someone you will have to treat with the utmost respect.

To some degree the Know-All is also a bluffer but there are clear distinctions. Whereas true bluffers do not set out to know what they are talking about, only to give other people that impression, the Know-Alls have a strong inner conviction that what they say is the last word on any given subject. It is particularly difficult to deal with people when they actually do know what they are talking about. You must learn to detect right away that you are not simply dealing with a fellow bluffer with possibly superior skills.

Tell-tale signs are that the Know-All:

– will not hesitate to talk to you as if you are a fool

– will have no sense of humour

– will often follow up with supporting facts, which bluffers carefully avoid doing

– will generally be on the right side of 50. After that age, as the memory begins to fade, Know-Alls almost imperceptibly become bluffers. And generally very good ones too.

Know-Alls tend to thrive most in practical, rather than artistic areas. They are particularly good on things like income-tax (paying and evasion of), insurance, business management in all its aspects, and holidays abroad.

What you must remember is that the Know-All is not an Expert. He or she has not indulged in anything as dreary as a lifetime's study of any particular subject, but simply garnered masses of superficial knowledge from such sources as *Which?*, *Reader's Digest*, consumer programmes, and anything in 36 fortnightly parts. They thus have a ready answer to almost anything. But they are easily ensnared here. Like most people, they take almost anything in print or on the air to be the gospel truth: because it comes from a remote source it is assumed to be wisdom beyond measure. What they forget is that most of these take-away articles and programmes are actually written (and/or presented) by bluffers.

An Expert, on the other hand, is a Know-All in one thing. His knowledge is therefore of greater depth and less easy to question. You will know an Expert because he will be able to tell you – indeed, will go out of his way to tell you – that even what you have read in the most learned sources (on his particular subject) is inaccurate. Get them off their subject right away.

HOW TO BECOME A
SUCCESSFUL BLUFFER

It is vital to accept that you cannot be an accomplished bluffer in everything. There are subjects such as crocodile-wrestling and sky-diving (where the motto which begins 'If at first you don't succeed' is of no practical use), which should be left to the expert. We suggest you make a start by taking on one Art, one Sport, one Social subject, one Leisure Activity. From these you can generally pick a subject that your opponent seems to have been at pains to avoid. If he starts off, for instance, by saying: 'Did you see Terry Wogan on television last night' (and there is a very good chance that he will say this) don't let him get settled into his diatribe. Counter by saying: "I rarely watch television – much too busy with my computer."

If he then shows signs of knowing something about computers or turns out to be Barry Norman who knows about computers and films, you need a well prepared exit route such as: "I think computers should be used but not heard about, don't you?" Then switch adroitly to: "What do you think of twelve-tone music?"

The chances are that having tested him already on three subjects, this is one that he may know nothing about. Nor do you, of course, but you have the basic facts from the appropriate book ready. We are not suggesting that these gambits have the makings of a good conversation.

Method

The essential thing to get right is the manner or style you adopt. Here are some of the classic methods:

The Question

Couch most of your remarks in the form of a question, particularly when on the defensive. Preface or terminate your most telling thrusts with the phrase "Don't you think ..?" This has a subtle element of conciliation without concession about it.

The Hedge

Never commit yourself totally. Use phrases like "I am inclined to think" and "Perhaps there is something to be said for..." You may then retract if you find you have gone too far in any direction.

The Look of Disbelief

Far be it for us to promote the cause of silence, but there is no doubt that the disbelieving or cynical look can be a major force – particularly if you happen to be at a loss for words.

Playing for Time

Less drastic, but highly effective: there is never any harm in saying that you "... will have to think it over". Even if, by some chance, you knew what you were talking about, it is quite a reasonable request.

Interjection

This can range from a quiet "Mmm" to a surprised "Oh!", a contemptuous snort, or a sardonic laugh. But by far the most effective is "Really?" in a questioning, even doubting, sort of tone. This can put some people off their stride and goad others into a state of fury.

The snort is an old and well-tried resort of the bluffer. It should not be overdone or it can appear merely vulgar; but done lightly, almost imperceptibly it can be extremely telling.

There is also the Grunt, in some ways even better than the Snort. Whereas snorts tend to be hostile and traditionally express contempt, the grunt has an indefinite quality about it and leaves your adversary in a very uncertain state of mind.

Ambiguity*

The whole essence of top-class bluffing is to make other people uncertain as to exactly what you mean. This can be achieved by the use of such phrases as "I used to think" which leaves it open as to whether you still do, or now don't.

Invention

This is perhaps the last resort of the resourceful bluffer, but nonetheless effective. To be successful it has to be carried out with complete conviction, or, if encountered in others, parried with equal enthusiasm. If someone says to you 'What do you think of Schwelschmann's Tuba Concerto?" (and you have reasonable doubts that Schwelschmann ever wrote anything for the tuba) simply reply "I greatly prefer the Mellophone Fantasia." He is then entrapped in his own invention.

---

* Some of the above are adapted from the excellent *Bluff Your Way in Philosophy* where they are applied to purely philosophical bluffing. But their application is so clearly universal that, with acknowledgement, we merely adapt them for general use.

Gesticulation

Anyone who has the facility for wild gestures has a useful weapon for diverting attention from what they are saying. The real art is to say one thing and gesticulate another. This can throw even the most practised of opponents.

Dress

It might not seem to be important or even relevant to bluffing but it is, in fact, quite an intrinsic part of the art. As Clewinson regularly maintained, no-one could win an argument against a man dressed in his pajamas. As pajama parties are often in vogue, this is a point well worth considering. Dress is important as camouflage or disguise; an effective way to throw people off balance. Take such obvious instances as a priest in mufti or a socialist politician smartly dressed. The practised bluffer will soon see through such sartorial trickery and can then use it to his own advantage by pretending to accept it at face value. It clearly supports Partridge's definition of a bluffer as 'an imposer who relies on an assumed appearance and speech'.

Props

Professor Hankinson* is a great champion of the pipe, and there is no doubt of its efficacy both as a time-waster and as a way of choking your opponent to

* In this instance we refer to Professor Jim Hankinson. The Hankinsons are a well-known family in bluffing circles.

death. Unfortunately pipe-smokers only account for some 2.387 per cent of the male population (though possibly more amongst philosophers) and the use of pipes seems to be almost negligible amongst females.

The more practical prop for the bluffer is the drink, whether it is alcoholic or not. Quite apart from various distracting ways of drinking it, dangerous threads can easily be broken by an apparently benevolent desire to refill your opponent's glass or, in real moments of crisis, refilling your own.

Delivery

Try to adopt a slow, measured and considered tone of voice, as if you knew what you were saying and had carefully thought it all out. This will give the effect of being assured (see Omniscient). The object is to brook no contradiction.

Failing this, there are a number of equally helpful alternatives. The following are various well-tried approaches or styles, mainly drawn from television and political sources, where bluffing has been developed to a fine art.

Sincere – As used by virtually all Prime and lesser Ministers. The normally demanding voice is made to sound smoothly unctuous.

Earnest or Serious – Used with success, in their heyday, by such figures as Enoch Powell and Norman Tebbit. It is very easy to be fooled by either, but don't attempt to be both sincere and earnest at the same time, or like them, you may well fail in both. Equally capable of carrying conviction.

Smiling – Can be a disaster as demonstrated by ex President Carter. For some reason it is frequently adopted by people who happen to have a lot of teeth, which compounds the error. But very disconcerting if timed to coincide with conversation about the most recent disaster, or the state of the economy.

Offensive (by which, of course we mean being on the offensive rather than just offensive; though they are frequently linked) – often used to great effect by television interviewers. Likewise by trades union leaders and Home Secretaries in a tight corner. The idea, basically, is to frighten the adversary without actually resorting to violence or even threat.

Overwhelming – As demonstrated by most Shadow Cabinet Ministers. Simply employ so many words, delivered at such a breathless pace, that your rival soon finds himself outplayed.

Omniscient –Inevitably successful, but does need a fair degree of confidence and the right sort of voice, confidential and controlled, such as possessed by Alistair Cooke. Nobody ever dreams of questioning what he says although, by his own admission, it is quite often of a bluffing nature and generally made up on the spur of the moment.

Cynical or mocking – As used by television intellectuals such as Barry Norman or Clive Anderson can be most effective, but can over-emphasise the bluffing content of your output. It pays to be suave as well in this instance, e.g. Noel Coward, who was a master of the art.

Nice – Generally works well because people are diffident about hurting the feelings of those who appear pleasant. It has been frequently used by Liberal leaders. The worried look, as used by John Major and Roy Jenkins has much the same putting off-guard sort of effect.

Innocent at large – Usefully employed by politicians who have recently been exposed by the press. A winner every time.

Eccentric – Fairly successful, at least as a temporary diversion. Effects used include facial contortion, hurried or impaired speech, and a foreign accent.

Bluff – Probably one of the best of all. The user pretends to be a good, honest soul, just like you or me. Supreme masters of the bluff approach are American Presidents who get themselves elected and even re-elected by this simple but wholly effective method.

GOOD BLUFFING SUBJECTS

The Arts

The arts have always provided quintessential bluffing material. One is bound, at some time, to be thrust into conversational combat with a fellow listener, reader or looker.

The principle thing to remember in artistic bluffing is that it is the superficial aspects of the art that matter, not the art itself.

Music

Outside the Academies (possibly inside them as well) nobody actually talks about the science of music, i.e. the notes and harmonies and all that sort of thing. Nor even about a specific piece of music. Can you imagine two average people comparing (to take an elementary example) Beethoven's 1st and 2nd Symphonies? Neither can we. If they are to touch upon Beethoven symphonies at all it will be to discuss So-and-So's performance of any given Beethoven symphony, and the appalling mess he made of it. Now that you can get your teeth into.

Anyone at a present-day concert or listening to a recording can tell that most performances are under-rehearsed, unwillingly undertaken and totally lacking in understanding. By the end of most performances, the performers will have used their professional expertise and televisual charm to persuade the audience that they are having a really enjoyable experience. The truth is that 86 per cent are not, and wish they were doing something else.

It is fortunate, in a way, that classical music as a living art is quite dead. 95 per cent of the public and performers are only interested in the music of the past. Only the outstanding 5 per cent would attend a programme of modern music, and most of those only because a living relative is involved. There is not much point, therefore, in the musical bluffer doing research on contemporary music as very few people are likely to discuss it, even in musical circles.

If you still want to talk about composers, then the only thing you really need to have up your sleeve is the names of the least known and least liked works. Trot these out with boring regularity.

Remember, too, that not all music is classical. You can score heavily in any company by a superficial knowledge of Jazz or, better still, some specialised area of jazz, like ragtime or the blues. It was an erstwhile red-nosed comedian, George Robey, who said that 'Jazz and all its attendant horrors are ruining home-life.' People, in view of his connections with mirth, laughed heartily at this. Had they seen the eventual results of the jazz invasion they would not so readily have regarded Mr. Robey as a bigoted and short-sighted old buffoon.

Jazz introduced a new language to music. It was no longer something that you could write down in a simple translatable form and then play in a correct manner, like *Just a Song at Twilight* or *The Maiden's Prayer*. It was improvised in a noisy and belligerent way. In this guise it went on to become the basis of all popular music from around November 1927 and especially what is known in today's abbreviated language as Pop.

There are two main kinds of Jazz: Traditional – the old sort with a tune, and Modern – the current sort without. To bop or not to bop – that is the question.

You can invent any number of jazz musicians with strange names, there are so many odd real ones that no-one will notice the difference.

Jazz is a sort of folk-music. Folk-music is that which wasn't written by anybody and was played by everybody – whether they were musical or not – and most of them weren't. It is always slightly off-key. Actually somebody must have written it and they were referred to as Anon. Eventually the Anons of the world got together and demanded payment; so Folk-music is now just as commercial as anything else.

You can always tell genuine folk-singers (to quote an erudite source) 'by the way they cup one ear in a hand and sing through their noses, thus leaving their mouths free for the passage of alcohol.' Most folk-singers come either from Newcastle-upon-Tyne or the Blue Ridge Mountains of Virginia.

As for Pop: first of all there was 'rock 'n' roll' which was boogie-woogie with a blues-type lyric added; then there was 'rhythm 'n' blues' (all pop singers say 'n') which was blues with a touch of boogie-woogie. After this pop just seemed to take over the air and went on 'n' on wherever you went, completely killing the art of conversation.

Pop groups proliferate at the rate of approximately 15 a day. Pop is incredibly popular and some people wear earphones all the time so as not to miss a note of it. This makes it very difficult to indulge in any normal sort of bluff. In fact, you may, in this area even indulge in a little hoodwinking and invent things.

Opera

This is an area where the bluffer should step warily as all opera fanatics are slightly odd, and aggressive.

To begin with they have the ability to appear absorbed in hours of tuneless incantation. They have, in fact, gone into a deep trance. This faculty is reflected in their conversational style, giving them the kind of unarguable blandness that you find when conversing with Tibetan monks and dedicated astrologers.

Opera poses several problems. If you really like music you are unlikely to want to have it spoilt by a lot of rather amateur actors wandering around a makeshift set in hired costumes. And if you like acting you would not choose to go to the opera over much for the above reasons, quite apart from the fact that opera plots are not often great shakes in terms of drama.

The basic plot of nine out of ten operas concerns a hero or heroine, or both, who live in a state of confusion, not realising that their lover is faithful though they appear not to be, or not recognising them at all because they are wearing a small mask. At the end they die of:

a) an over-high note
b) inexplicable grief
c) T.B.

The answer might be to listen to opera on records but this is not always satisfactory. Because of the strain of having to set all those words to music, the scores come up on the average with only one good tune per opera. The better ones may have more – possibly two or three. A dedication to the golden voices of the past can be counteracted by an equally untenable belief in present-day singers, or vice versa.

No opera-seria can ever be taken seriously; no opera comique is very comical; and Wagner is a very specialised taste. You are advised to steer clear of anything to do with Bayreuth.

Theatre

There are still several good reasons for going to the Theatre, but they all return to the same thing, namely: so that you can say you have been to the Theatre.

The acting profession is just one long bluff from start to finish (see Four Key Qualities) so that anything you say, provided you say it with enough authority, will carry you through.

Art

Most people only see what they think they see. They are very susceptible therefore to being persuaded that what they think they see is not what they ought to see. Or what they ought to see is what some bluffer or other thinks they ought to see. It's the ideal field to be in.

If you are standing in front of a large canvas which is entirely black except for a small red blob in one corner and the expert says 'How profound', you can only agree. The artist may have titled this masterpiece, which is being offered for sale at a mere 7,500, *Thoughts Before Conception*. You will find it difficult to disagree with that as well. Likewise when you come across a small pile of pebbles in a gallery labelled *United Nations*. Or a lump of stone with a hole in the middle called *Miscarriage*. But do not be daunted. When you get into real art, the older sort of thing, words like 'arrangement', 'perspective', 'depth', 'intransigence', 'balance' and 'balderdash' are all yours for the asking.

In the field of Modern Art you merely use a more modern vocabulary – 'obvious', 'viable', 'knickers', and so on. Once you get into the swing of it, your bluff is as good as anyone else's.

Literature

Unlike Music and Art, Literature can, to some degree, be indulged in by most people. It is simply a matter of reading. As a result most people think they know something about it and lots of them even write it.

Pre-eminent in literature is Shakespeare, who wrote an enormous amount. Some of his plays are known to everyone because they are so full of quotations. He invented a sort of linguistic affectation that could make complete nonsense sound very profound, e.g. 'Ann hath a way with her that doth nip the portals of my soul like the pincers of a half-baked lobster.' That sort of thing has been fruitful grounds for interpretation and scholastic research ever since. This is why, however much you feel like snorting, you should treat the name with the utmost reverence.

Or you could profess admiration for the new vogue for presenting Shakespeare (or anyone else) in strip-cartoons. Few will know how to refute your claim that these are "Very progressive". Some people even rank Shakespeare with God and say they don't believe he existed at all.

After Shakespeare come all the classics. These are the writers that no one actually reads, except when they have to. Names like Chaucer, Milton, and Spenser – particularly Spenser. A line learned from somewhere deep in the latter portion of one of their longer poems, where no man has ever trod, will prove beyond doubt that you are well up in literary life.

Rating only slightly below these, are the well-loved classics. These are the ones most people have read bits of – like Dickens and Tennyson; generally of a later date and therefore more linguistically accessible. The thing here is not to go for the obvious like *Oliver*

Twist or *David Copperfield*, both of which have been filmed, but to read a chapter (no need to go further than that) of *Our Mutual Friend* or *Little Doritt*.

The rest of literature may be rated according to its readability. Top marks go to those which are virtually unreadable (e.g. James Joyce, Samuel Beckett); bottom to those which are readily understandable. If they also happen to be enjoyable then the shrugged shoulder or a Leavis-like smile is all that is necessary; although it doesn't make for good conversation.

People who have become blatantly popular like Ian Fleming, Agatha Christie, William Burroughs, or John Betjeman, can now be discussed as folk-art and given some status (but not too much) in this new light.

Business

There are many areas of human activity where the whole structure of social behaviour and working relations is based on the art of bluffing; not applied with any malicious intent, but simply as a means of self-preservation. Thus it is in the Business world, which is entirely founded on bluff.

Business is, by its very nature, the act of kidding someone, whether it be a colleague above or below you in the same business, or someone in another business to whom you want to sell something or from whom you buy something, into a belief that a) you know what you are doing, and b) are to be trusted. Anyone in business will know how difficult this is in the face of the fact that a) it is blatantly obvious that you don't know what you are doing, and b) you would cheerfully sell bad eggs to your grandmother.

It is essential, if relationships are to be maintained and business is to be done, to make the utmost effort to get away with it and, need we say it, the only way is by building a well-balanced edifice of bluff.

Business splits itself into various ill-defined areas of activity, one of which you will have to choose as your main bluffing province, with a fringe bluffing knowledge of all the others, most of which you will have to cope with at some time or other. Some of the most important are:

Accountancy – The art of proving, by some means or other a) that the books balance; b) that the business is in working order; c) that too much tax is being paid; and d) that you are worthy of your high fees or salary. Not necessarily in that order.

Economics – The science behind Accountancy for which most accountants seem to show a distinct lack of appreciation.

Finance – The practical way of convincing everyone that you know what you are doing and can be trusted. And make a profit out of it, in spite of the accountant.

Computers – The justification for substantial reductions in traditional staff in order to be able to employ additional staff to cope with all the extra work that is caused by the supplanting of fallible employees by fallible machines (see Computers below).

Management – The art of proving to those who work under you that you know what you are doing. There is no point in spending time in trying to convince anyone that you can be trusted.

Marketing – The art of getting what you sell to the people who want to buy it. Success in this may reluctantly convince them that you know what you are doing.

Advertising – The art of convincing the people who might want to buy something, that they ought to get it.

Public Relations – The art of convincing everyone that you can be trusted. In spite of the fact that you clearly don't know what you are doing.

Salesmanship – Proving that, although you probably can't be trusted, you do know what you are doing.

Once all these facets of Business, and their attached bluffology have been mastered you will be well equipped to repent immediately and enter the Church.

Computers

Practised bluffers of the top rank should be able to sail their way through most subjects. But even they will be facing a demanding trial of strength that may well prove to be their downfall when the talk veers, as it may well do in this age of hardware (and hardware is no longer what you thought it was), to the world of computers.

The main point to remember is that no-one over thirty is able to comprehend computer jargon, and very few even in the twenty-to-thirty bracket. Children under fifteen converse naturally on the subject, so never enter into conversation with a child. The other group to watch out for carefully are computer experts;

but they are by no means invulnerable as many of them are over thirty. They can also be baffled by simple, straightforward questions and, as few of them have any sense of humour, they are easily floored by flippancy.

It is not so much that you need to know about computers as that you need to surmount the language barrier. It is possible for a normally intelligent person to read the whole of the computer section of *The Guardian* on Thursday, or any computer magazine or manual (the latter obviously translated from the Korean by a Czech) without understanding a single word of it. But this, in fact, is the Achilles heel of the computer world. There are now so many names and jargon terms that the usually weak ruse of inventing a few more can be highly successful.

Should you, by a stroke of good fortune, have come up against an uncertain bluffer in the computer field, launch into a heartless attack on the claims he is making for his new Atari by comparing it with your new Aristotle – the thinking man's machine.

Before your victim has time to cast doubts on the Aristotle's validity (which they can hardly do, if you firmly say that you own one – for it might well be a model introduced only last week) you must move on to say that you went for the Aristotle not only for its cheapness and its fail-safe interlinear anti-espionage device (it also uses the new take-away chips) but because it offers a full Japanese-planned pull-down menu. No 64K RAM for you, you say, laughingly. You go for the 32 Mb BUM which lets you link up with the micro-Bollocs business system and offers the possibility of up-grading to the new author-orientated EvenSofta software. You would go on, but won't, except to say that it is the first machine not to be troubled by mice.

It seems that nearly all computers up to now have had a mouse in them – which seems to be asking for trouble. Computer operators seem to have had mice like old-time comedians had mothers-in-law. It is no use having a machine handling 16 megabytes directly if a lot of mice are going to have first nibble.

There is a danger that, by this time, your adversary may have realised that you are a raving lunatic. If you sense that he is about to make a comeback on behalf of his Atari, quickly make it clear that you have lost interest in the subject. Casually say some-thing like: "I bet you didn't know that in 1888 Theophilus van Kammel invented the revolving door."

Sports

Starting with Poker (as cited in our introductory pages) most card games are the art of bluffing translated into visual reality. There is virtually no card game (with the possible exception of Snap) that is not based on the art of making your opponent believe that you possess something which you don't. If this is vitally true of Poker, Bridge, Vingt-et-Un, etc., it goes all the way down to Happy Families and is what bluffing is all about. We would go so far as to say that a working knowledge of card games is an essential asset to the bluffer who wishes to be fully equipped.

It is in the Club Sports that bluffing moves into a more social aspect. The thing here, of course, is that belonging to a Club is of greater significance than the Sport around which it revolves. It is a world of blazers and ties, AGMs and many Committees, precedental standing and admission to the bar only in proper dress.

Much the same rules apply to most Clubs. Tennis is a comparatively friendly example where the pecking order can be bent slightly on the strength of a drink or two. That is because the British are not very good at Tennis and don't take it too seriously. But there are games that are so important, practically religions, that you might well deem it wise to become a specialist in them alone – for example Cricket and Golf. Others such as Polo are beyond our means and comprehension.

Cricket

It is important to remember that cricket was a very special game invented by and for the English. So they couched its terms and rules in a language that they felt no one else would understand; most of it based on early or middle Anglo-Saxon. To take a very simple example: the side that are 'in' take it in turns to get 'out'. You know when someone is 'out' because they then come back in. The bowler's turn to throw the ball is known as an 'over' even before he has begun. For many years these sorts of ruses fooled most foreigners and non-English speaking nations never even tried to play it. Imagine how ridiculous it would sound in French having to say 'qu'est que c'est que ca?' instead of the graceful and succinct English 'howzat?'

But gradually people like the Australians got the hang of it and took it up. For some time the English continued to win against these other nations by not letting them know what was meant by 'silly mid-on' and 'yorker' but the wily colonials eventually found these things out and began to triumph. Today it is considered a matter for national rejoicing if England manage to win a Test Match or two.

In England there is a fairly snobbish set-up called County Cricket. This causes hard feeling because only a selected number of teams are allowed to call themselves first-class counties and to be seen on television on Sunday afternoons. Unlike Soccer, where clubs can fight their way into the First Division, first-class cricket seems to be forever barred to second-class counties like Cheshire and Lincolnshire (though Durham somehow managed to slip through), all Welsh counties except Glamorgan, and the whole of Scotland because of their kilts.

While cricket was mainly in the safe hands of English gentlemen (Amateurs and Professionals) it supposedly was a game in which good manners and fair play predominated. Hence the phrase 'not cricket' was applied to anything otherwise. But this and other terms like 'clean-bowled' have fallen into disuse as cricket has become an ill-mannered and even violent game more akin to boxing. The aim of the bowler is now to hit and fell the batsman who is forced to come to the wicket in ever increasing amounts of armour.

Conversational bluffing on the subject of cricket is almost entirely on knowledge assimilated from those thick and turgid tomes edited by Norman Wisden, which give the statistics of every important match played since 1066. One has to be able to say, without hesitation, what record opening partnership was achieved by Grace and Faver in 1857 or how many Tests England won in 1931. It may well reveal your age, but it is effective to be able to say that you saw Hammond bat and Larwood bowl. But don't try to impress by saying that you saw Bradman's last innings. Everyone claims that privilege, though they all seem to have watched different matches.

Golf

This is a multi-facetted and devious subject. There are various levels on which to talk about it. Such as:

a) The Playing of Golf, its Dress and Quaint Rituals. At almost any gathering you will meet someone who plays, has played or is about to play Golf. In the first instance, with a fellow golfer, you will experience the pathetic eagerness of a fellow-sufferer anxious to lay bare his soul. It doesn't really matter much what you say or what stories you tell as the other person will not be listening. You will both be talking at the same time, explaining how you came to miss the 15th green on Friday and how it somehow went all wrong after that.

In the second instance, the ex-player, the situation will be much the same. He will be telling you how he missed the 15th green in 1963 – and how it somehow went all wrong after that. It was only after his second divorce that he gave up golf.

It is the third instance that holds most promise – the one about to take up golf. You need feel no restraint in offering advice as to how they can set about achieving perfection, meanwhile getting rid of several hundred pounds and ruining their marriage. Sell them your old clubs.

b) Other People Playing Golf.
You soon get involved in a savage appraisal of the top professionals Their occasional errors are reminiscent of your more frequent ones, so you can talk with confidence. Better, of course, to have been there so that you can tell them what Tony Jacklin said to you (after you had clicked your camera as he was in mid-swing). Enough that he spoke at all.

c) The Psychology of Golf.

This is not often discussed at its deepest level. Players may be prepared to analyse their reasons for not playing well, but rarely their reasons for playing it at all. They are fully aware that it is injurious to the health, both physically and mentally. They are fully aware that it has made them selfish, arrogant, spendthrift, stupidly optimistic, etc. If someone explained to them why they did it, they almost certainly wouldn't.

Leisure and Hobbies

It is where people step away from the cut and thrust of business and work and into the fantasy world of their hobbies and leisure pursuits that some of the most potent bluffing comes into action. It is here, even if their employment is of the lowliest (an author or musician even) that everyone becomes an expert or what is known as an enthusiast. Be it gardening, boating, skiing, stamp-collecting, wine – wise bluffers should see to it that they don't become entangled with an enthusiast.

Enthusiasts are so obsessed with their obsessions that they have little mind for anything else. Whereas the more generalised bluffer will ease his way into a conversation with some vague chat about the weather, the traffic or the latest trade figures (he might, of course, be a weather, traffic or trade figure expert, so be careful), the specialised enthusiast will take one look at you and, if he considers you mug enough, will plunge right in with some remark like "Do you garden?", "Seen any good penny blacks lately?" or "Badly kept wine, this." The answer to the first two is either "No" or "Oh", and to the last "Isn't that Leslie Clutterhouse over there? Haven't seen him for years. Must go and have a chat. Scuse me."

If really cornered by an enthusiast the best thing is to be totally deaf or claim an allergy. If you happen to have read the appropriate Bluffer's Guide, of course, you will stay and accept the challenge.

DIY

A popular area for home bluffing is DIY. There are basically two kinds of DIYers. Those who can and those who can't. This applies to everything from knocking in a nail to building a house.

The DIYers who can't are rather pathetic. They take to DIY either because they imagine they are among the 'cans' (in which case you are called upon to admire various crooked shelves, botched wall-papering and lethal electrics: or, because they can't afford to GSETDIFY (Get Someone Else To Do It For You). In this case they might try to pretend that the shelves and electrics are not DIY at all. The practised eye will soon detect that the wallpaper is on upside-down and that hot water is coming out of the cold tap and gas out of the hot. But you could be fooled here as there are plenty of plumbers around capable of the same miscalculations.

Good DIYers are impossible. They will try to coax you (and you will do the same if you are one) into boundless admiration of that which they have just DIYed. "But it must have cost thousands" they/you are expected to murmur in response to the cajoling. "No, we did it ourselves" (DIO) is the immodest answer.

It is your bounden duty to deflate DIYers, whether good or bad. If they are good they are unbearable; if they are bad they are dangerous. When shown a newly tiled bathroom, do not hesitate to rap the tiles with the knuckle and say "but these are plastic" or (even worse) "embossed paper". Poke or pull anything you can and if it comes off you are in a strong position. After you have detached a few drawer handles and torn down a switch or two the DIYer will begin to lose confidence. If you are a bad DIYer yourself then make sure that recent lines of demarcation are well covered by strategically placed houseplants.

GSETDIFY

The confirmed GSETDIFY is, on the other hand, either rich or bone idle. The sort of man who would marry a woman with six children to save himself the effort.

The GSETDIFYer is probably even more unbearable than the DIYer. Lightly dropped remarks such as "We simply asked Harrods to do the lot" are calculated to make one pay one's Communist Party dues on the spot. However, the GSETDIFYer will have suffered quite a bit while it was all in motion. Everyone knows about the electrician who tears up the floorboards only to find it's the wrong room; the roofer who puts his foot through the sound bit; and the tree-feller who creates work for the roofer. And the endless cups of tea.

The bluffing interplay is at its most virulent in these areas. Faced with a DIYer one immediately assumes the mantle of a condescending GSETDIFYer; faced with a smug GSETDIFYer one becomes an arrogant DIYer.

Some ready phrases to use as appropriate: "You don't mean to say you paid all that, for that?"; "How do you find the time?", "We are so rarely at home", and "Should it really be that way round?

Fitness

Being fit has become such a preoccupation with modern society that you have to take a positive attitude towards it. It is no use being half and half. Either you declare that you are dedicated to keeping fit – in which case you have a great deal of bluffing to do as only 10 per cent of the population are fully fit, and most of those are under 6. Or you declare that you've never had a day's illness in your life, a pose that will infuriate most people beyond coherence – particularly if it happens to be true, but of course that isn't necessary.

The average person has something wrong with them somewhere most of the time. The only days when they feel 100 per cent fit is just before a cold comes on. It is therefore even more effective if you can link your robust health with the don't care attitude, and claim that, like Churchill, you believe in "eating, drinking and smoking to excess as the recipe for a long and active life."

Sex

The bluffing areas of sex are mainly in the run up to it under such various headings as Expectations, Titillation, Cost-Efficiency, Crikey and There Was I Waiting at the Church. It is in these areas that the art of the bluffer is most profitably expended. It can be so effectively deployed that successful bluffers can earn a reputation without actually getting down to it at all. That is if they want it that way. Or any of the other ways, of which there are so many. Talking about sex can almost be as satisfying as the real thing, and not half so risky.

Everyone throughout life is deeply concerned with the art of sex bluffing. Everyone. Even monks and nuns. In fact, especially monks and nuns. Even elderly ladies at Conservative garden parties.

As with most subjects that we have dallied with herein, there seem to be just two main schools of thought on the matter of sex as an adjunct to Life. You either believe, as apparently most film directors do, that sex is everything, the prime motive for living, or you believe that all that long, involved, tiring, expensive business of seduction often seems hardly worth the brief moment of pleasure that is the end result.

Sex is one of those indeterminate areas of human activity where you are never quite sure who you are bluffing – yourself or the other person. Assuming that you belong, as most people do, to the second group, but that you feel the need to impress somebody whom you think might be a film director, then these are some good lines to try out:

a) that you first tried to have sex at the age of six months, but that the pram tipped over.
b) that you first thought of getting married at the age of nine but decided just to live with him/her instead.
c) that your first proper partner was very impressed by what you had to offer. But not in the other prospects.
d) that you can take it or leave it.

Languages

Surmounting language barriers has required a skilled application of the bluffer's art since the beginning of history. The first tourists in any country were usually uninvited and heavily armed. The Roman legionnaire only trying to be friendly with the early English would say something like: 'Ohum, quellum bellum dayum.' The indignant native, assuming quite rightly that the soldier was only trying to get off with his daughter, would reply in Anglo-Saxon 'Why don't you bugger off?' leaving the Roman to try and make sense of 'Bugga? Buggamis? Buggatis?' in that declining way the Romans had, and go sadly on his way.

As every tourist knows, the principle way to communicate with a foreigner is to treat him as if he was deaf and daft and to speak very loudly and slowly, occasionally adding an 'a' to the end of the principal nouns. But this has problems. The truly foolproof way you can bluff anybody into believing that you know a language, when you don't, is to greet the hostile in his or her own tongue with the equivalent of 'Hi', for courtesy's sake, and promptly declare yourself to be:

- Dutch in France
- Swedish in the Middle East
- Lithuanian everywhere else.

You then suggest, in broken, halting English that each of you use English to communicate.

Politics

Another first-rate subject for bluffing, not least because it seems to be about 99.9 per cent bluff in the first place. Nobody actually believes in politics, least of all those involved in it. The whole point of talking about politics, and inevitably revealing your political leanings, is not to garner admiration for your convictions or even to promote them, but to establish your character, position and degree of success in life.

The Conservative party has a good deal going for it; the support of those who enjoy affluence and power; the backing of the popular press; and best of all, no actual policies to pursue beyond a belief in the status quo, i.e. those who have, keep, and those who haven't, hard luck. Thus the main line of bluffing, from a right-wing point of view is to put up a good pretence of caring for those less fortunate than yourself. This gives the impression that you are more successful than you really are.

The Labour or Socialist line in politics is more difficult to maintain because it is inclined to involve definite policies firmly based on such basic things as dislike and envy. But the bluffer can make good profit out of the assumption that being left-wing makes one rather more intelligent, deeper thinking, more caring than average.

The best opportunities come with middle-of-the-way parties like the Liberals. Belonging to these means that one can profess some sort of social conscience and vague leanings towards the left while preferring to live a predominantly right-wing, conservative, kind of life. It can be assumed that most genuine bluffers belong to this twilight zone of the uncommitted. It puts them in a position to be able to argue both ways. The whole basis of political argument is that faced with a diehard rightist you tend to take a stance well to the left, or faced with a leftist, well to the right. With care you still end up astride the fence of life and prove yourself to be liberal in the best and least political sense of the word.

It must be remembered that political argument has no influence whatever on political thought. Those who don't know or don't think may be persuaded to switch allegiance according to what is on offer, but the politically convicted are unchangeable.

There are some people around who upset the generally acceptable pattern of political behaviour. There are, for example, the .1 per cent who really do believe in something and are not bluffing. If you meet one of these it is best to edge away as quickly as possible.

You should be careful, too, not to be fooled by appearances. The man in the pin-striped suit who gives every appearance of having been to Eton may well turn out to have sharply leftist views. Likewise the impoverished looking old bloke with soup-stains down his front might well turn out to be one of the aristocracy. This is calculated bluffing at its best, and you will find here an adversary worthy of your best efforts.

Class

There is no area of human in-fighting where bluffing is more necessary or effective than in jolly old class warfare. Start by ignoring all attempts to convince you that class is non-existent and that you are just a snob. Class is man's lifeline; even though he may use it at times to hang himself. Without class he would not know what his station in life was – be it Euston, Exeter or Glasgow Central.

One does not discuss class in bluffing circles so much as use it as a foil. Firstly, when speaking to someone, you have to decide what class they are. If you can get that right you are in a strong position either to anticipate their answers or to annoy them by a wrong assumption of their position in life. But, of course, it isn't easy and classwatching is a demanding study. Even an Earl can have bad breath and there's many a man entitled to call himself Sir who holds up his trousers with a tie. Attitudes to class change. Only noticeably every hundred years or so – but they change.

Up to about 1857 the working-class were always considered to be either comical, criminal or half-witted – or all three – and were thus portrayed in all books, operas and paintings. In the age of enlightenment that followed it was recognised that they could be a nuisance as well and had a vote. At the other extreme, it has always been held that the upper class are inclined to be woozy and prematurely senile. Television exposure of their activities in the House of Lords has confirmed this. But at least they all appear to be genuinely sorry for what they did in the past. The middle classes are always looking upwards and wanting to be thought a degree higher than they are.

This, of course, is their Achilles heel. This is where you pounce and begin to shatter their carefully-built image. As Evelyn Waugh said, discover that a man is fond of cider and tinned salmon and you have discovered that his background is agricultural.

Most people are middle-class, though with fine shades of distinction. The difference between upper and lower middle-class, for example, is revealed by which newspapers they use as underfelt; or whether they roast, boil or fry their potatoes. Other things as well but these are the important ones.

All bluffers should proceed on the belief that they are the only person in the world who is truly classless. And never forget that women are twice as classy as men.

INTERNATIONAL BLUFF

We were only slightly rocked back on our heels the other day when an incredibly serious man from the BBC said that he didn't think much of The Bluffer's Guides because they were full of sweeping generalisations. Our shaken retort, quite unworthy of a true bluffer, was that sweeping generalisations were the life-blood of bluffing. 'Oh', he said.

It is therefore in an unrepentant spirit that the following generalisations concerning other nations are made.

Americans

Americans are marvellous people – generous, sincere, concerned and democratic. You will find them hard to bluff as they have a natural flair for it themselves. They are always coming out with innocently clever remarks, like the one, the other day, who described the English as the only people who apologised when you trod on their toes. Not only do they freely use the word 'bluff' but it seems it might well have originated there.

Australians

Australian men are big and burly and are very fond of beer. Australian women are even bigger and burlier and employed in opera. Australia, apart from the bits round the edges, is mainly empty spaces inhabited by kangaroos. Australians are therefore bluff by nature.

French

The French are utterly untrustworthy and spend most of their time trying to do-down the British. They know all about bluffing. The French for bluff is 'le bluff', bluffer is 'le bluffer' and the verb is 'faire de bluff'. If we are not careful they will claim that we took the word from them.

Germans

The Germans, as we all know, are not to be trusted, and have spent quite a lot of their time trying to do-down the British. They are very good at poker. The German for bluff is 'der Bluff' and the verb is 'bluffen' or 'verbluffen'. It looks like everyone is trying to get in on the act.

Spanish

The Spanish are untrustworthy and think they ought to own Gibraltar – which could be described as a bluff at the south-west extremity of Spain. The Spanish for 'bluff' is the wonderful word 'fanfarronada' the verb is fanfarronear, and a bluffer is a fanfarrón. They are said to be able to fanfarronade their way out of anything.

Italians

The Italians are not to be trusted as they live entirely on spaghetti and similar forms of pasta, washing it down with their best wine which they keep for themselves. They never bluff but are always in deadly earnest. Their word for bluff is 'millaneria' and a bluffer is a 'millantatore'. When they stick a knife in you they mean it.

Swiss

The Swiss are a race of bankers and clock-makers, clinging to the sides of a country full of high mountains which foreigners have a passion for sliding down. Their staple diet is a tasteless cheese full of holes. They bluff their way along very nicely thank you and switch with ease from 'le bluff' to 'der bluff' and even millantarsi' before you have come to grips with them. In view of all this, they are probably not to be trusted.

Jews

The Jews were the subject of all jokes before they were ousted by the Scots and latterly by the Irish. The Jewish way of life is based on bluff and counter-bluff and they invented The Bluffer's Guides – so don't get involved in any argument here.

Japanese

It is said that the Japanese are not to be trusted and will pinch any ideas we happen to have. They spend their time trying to out-do or under-price everybody. We are unable, on our antiquated word processor, to show you what the Japanese for bluff is, but you can be sure it is closely modelled on ours. And they are masters of the art.

All other races are untrustworthy.

A CONTHOLOGY

The Cunning Kind of Bluff

Bluffing is no easy matter. It requires skill, dedication, attention to detail, and utter conviction in order to scale the heights of true inter-personal fraudulence. But it's well worth the effort: people will look at you in a new light; the Smart set will invite you to their dinner parties; beautiful women and handsome men will start cultivating your friendship, and temptresses and gigolos of international repute will slide seductively between the sheets*...

Bluffing has always been so integral a part of everybody's life, in all lands, at all levels, that it is essential to name some of the heroes, recount some of their exploits, and draw such lessons as you can from their triumphs. As Len Deighton says somewhere: 'There isn't a man, woman or child in this world who can say they have never conned someone out of something. Babies smile for a hug, girls for a mink, men for an empire.'

Here, by way of an aperitif, are a few random examples of the bluffer in action in recent times.

Great Bluffers

• In the 1920s, a Czech nobleman got hold of some impressive French government notepaper and used it to invite bids for the Eiffel Tower, to be sold as scrap metal, seven thousand tons of the stuff. Within two months he had sold it twice.

*Though we can't actually guarantee that this will take place.

• A journalist, Mr Peter Bryan, bluffed his way into the Olympic village in Tokyo simply by wearing his 1948 Olympic blazer. When they found out about this the Japanese authorities, anxious to save face, refused to let him leave on the inscrutable grounds that because he shouldn't be there he couldn't be there and if he wasn't there, how could they let him out?

• When he died in 1976 in a Chicago nursing home at the age of 100, Joseph 'Yellow Kid' Weill was widely acclaimed as the greatest of America's conmen. Serious students rate the claims of Wilson Mizner (*q.v*) very much higher but Weill was certainly assiduous and inventive. He sold 'talking dogs' that could not talk. He loaded a shotgun with pellets of gold, fired them into the wall of a disused quarry and sold shares in his 'goldmine'. He treated a stretch of the Colorado River in a similar manner and flogged the panning rights. It was reckoned that altogether he must have netted some 4 million. He served six years in prison. Weill was credited with two statements: 'I never play bingo, it's a rip-off' and: 'I never fleeced anyone who could not afford my price for a lesson in honesty.'

Which raises an issue that now has to be faced...

It must already be clear that any survey of Great Bluffers has to deal for the most part with men (it has mostly been men) who have gone, in legal and ethical terms, too far. They have let neither the social decencies nor legal penalties deter them in their pursuit of power, women, promotion, social standing, fame, gain, glory or anything else that seemed desirable to them at the time.

So the shocking fact is that those who succeeded –

or failed – on such a scale that they are remembered in the history books were (with a few exceptions) ruffians and thugs, charlatans and heartless deceivers, swindlers, forgers, coney-catchers, hornswogglers, humbugs, four-flushers, cheats and cozeners, quacks and imposters, frauds, fakes and dissemblers, with scarcely two moral scruples to rub together among the whole rogues' gallery of them.

Of course, it is no part of the aims of the Bluffer's Guides to encourage this sort of behaviour. The cunning and the criminal who invest these pages are not set up as examples. But the gentle, serious, social buffer, the natural student of this series, may learn something from their styles and techniques and fates.

Most of those who have made a career out of bluffing claim that the folk they dupe are the victims of their own greed and stupidity. There is justification for this. The 'gull' is offered the chance of easy and shady money. He jumps at it. He loses his investment and cannot complain since he has been involved in illegality himself. That is the general pattern and it can be argued that there is a salutary moral effect – the victim goes back to the honest life 'a sadder and wiser man'. But to go further and claim, as 'Yellow Kid' Weill did, that he was merely giving lessons in good behaviour and never over-charged for them is blatant bluff and nonsense. It is impossible to imagine any self-respecting conman pausing, in mid action to find out if his victim can really afford the price that's being exacted – and holding back if the answer is no. The conman's code of conduct is based on simple maxims:

- There's one born every minute.
- Never give a sucker an even break.
- Take 'em for all you can.

It is all most reprehensible, but the use of this kind of bluff has received support from some very weighty quarters.

Nicolo Machiavelli, the beady-eyed theorist of power politics in 16th century Italy, stated in his master-work *The Prince*:

> It is necessary to be a great pretender and dissembler; men are so simple and so subject to present necessities that he who seeks to deceive will always find someone who will allow himself to be deceived... The vulgar are always taken in by what a thing seems to be.'

These are lapidary injunctions and should be repeated regularly, by all aspiring bluffers. Machiavelli points to the root truth from which all bluffing springs – the fact that most folk are honest and ingenuous and gullible, quite happy to accept you at your own estimation of yourself. It always pays to pitch it strong.

Winston Churchill too, was all for bluff and deception. 'It is not for democracy', he said when he was congratulated on the allied landings in North Africa, 'to emulate the oyster, serene in its grotto, but rather the blur and smear of the cuttle fish with its dissembling inky fluid.'

The accomplished bluffer, for all his moral shortcomings, earns the affection of all. He is envied and respected for his skill, his cleverness, his gallant impudence. Even those who have themselves been horribly bluffed will, after some time, come round and admit their admiration.

It must therefore be acknowledged that the deceptive form of bluff calls for noble and admirable qualities.

Four Key Qualities

1. A Quick Wit and a Ready Tongue

A fine example of this appears in the Marx Brother's film *A Day at the Races* when **Groucho**, playing Dr. Hackenbush, is challenged to prove that he really is a medical man. He seizes a nearby wrist, peers intently at his watch for a few seconds and delivers the clinching line: 'Either this man is dead or my watch has stopped.'

Example 2. **Horatio Bottomley,** a little fat man with a taste for ostentatious living (champagne, expensive suits, eminent acquaintances) who had made his wealth by taking small sums off many thousands of folk in return for worthless shares and bonds, was eventually overtaken by the law and ended up in Wormwood Scrubs.

A visitor to his prison cell found him sewing mailbags and remarked 'Ah, Bottomley, sewing?' 'No,' came the reply, 'reaping.'

Example 3. The essayist **Charles Lamb** (who has the unique distinction of once having made William Wordsworth laugh) spent all his long working life on a high stool in a boring office in the City. He hated it and, approaching retirement, did little to hide his feelings. One day his boss summoned him and ticked him off fiercely: 'Do not think', he shouted, 'that I have failed to notice how late you are arriving for work in the mornings.'

'But have you not also noticed,' Lamb replied 'how early I depart in the afternoons?'

This is also a good example of the effectiveness of the lateral thought which, by sheer unexpectedness and its power to bewilder, can stop a challenger dead in his tracks.

All the great bluffers had it in great measure. The Master, Wilson Mizner, asked by a magistrate if he was trying to show contempt for the court, replied 'No, I'm trying to conceal it.'

It is sometimes an effective ploy, when being pressed closely, to answer an awkward question with another question, raising wider philosophical considerations. The first recorded attempt at this was made by Cain who, having just murdered his brother Abel, was confronted by the Lord and asked where Abel was. 'Am I my brother's keeper?' (*Genesis* chap. 4, verse 9) was the famous response. It did not work in this case but it was, in the circumstances, a damn good try. Even the most accomplished of bluffers can hardly hope to get away with it when up against outright omniscience.

2. Sheer Audacity

A hero of P.G. Wodehouse, Stanley Featherstonehaugh Ukridge, explains his philosophy in these words:

'Laddie, there's one thing that'll carry you through any mess.'

'And that is...?'

'Cheek, my boy, cheek. Gall. Nerve.'

One of the few endearing things known about the dervishes of Persia is that they lived on the principle that you can achieve anything by audacity. This is a fundamental tenet of the bluffer's faith based on two self-evident facts: that the great majority of people will believe almost anything, and that the more outrageous the claim, the more they will be inclined to accept it.

Example 1. Perhaps the best example, among many, took place in 1805 on the great wooden bridge across the Danube at Spitz. The French were on the southern banks of the river but Austrian infantry and artillery held the northern side, and their engineers had fixed explosives so the bridge could be destroyed at the first hint of an attack.

The problem of getting across without getting either shot or wet (or both) was solved by two of Napoleon's young Marshals from Gascony, Murat and Lannes. They put on their full-dress uniforms and rode slowly over the bridge in broad daylight, chatting together and with no sign of an escort. The astonished Austrians held their fire. Their commander, Prince Auersperg, who was old and uncommonly foolish, met them at the northern end and asked what was going on. 'Haven't you heard of the armistice?' they said. 'It's just been signed and the bridge has been handed to us.'

A long and friendly discussion followed in the course of which French sappers crept up under cover and uncoupled the fuses. Prince Auersperg was finally persuaded and ordered his men to retire. When one of his sergeants expressed dissent, Murat cried: 'Is this your famous Austrian discipline, where sergeants countermand the orders of a general?' The sergeant was put under arrest. Lannes sat on the barrel of an

Austrian gun to prevent it being levelled. And when the French grenadiers began to march across the bridge and even Auersperg started to suspect something, the Gascons* reassured him with the words: 'They're not advancing – just marking time to keep their feet warm'.

Example 2. Newspapers such as the *News of the World* and *The Sun*, are the favourite targets of one of today's most active bluffers, **Michael 'Rocky' Ryan**. He has made a highly successful speciality of getting the British press, usually at the 'gutter press' end of the business, to print completely groundless stories. His ground rules are simple:

a) The story must be absolutely untrue. He goes to great lengths to make sure of this. He would not dream of dealing with any story that had the least taint of factual accuracy.

b) It must be the sort of story that would appeal to the depraved and tendentious tastes of news editors.

'It's too easy', Ryan says, 'You just have to give them something they *want* to believe.'

3. Acting Skill

Bluffers are in the pretence business and the best bluffers employ every artifice of costume, body language and intonation to impose the illusion. Some have been so accomplished that they have begun to believe their own bluff, but that is extremely dangerous. Bluffing is something you do to others – never to yourself.

* Unsurprisingly, to 'gasconnade' is to talk big, boastingly, bluffingly.

Certain manners and expressions are particularly valuable. They may be categorised as follows:

Expression 1. **The air of authority**. This is the essential one and all the great bluffers have had it at their command:

• Mr. **Bernard Levin**, before he became rich and famous as a gadfly journalist, helped to make ends meet by guiding parties of tourists round the historic sites of London. Gazing at the Horse Guards one day, an American matron said, 'Tell me, what are they guarding?' Without a moment's hesitation and with exactly the right weight of quiet authority, Levin replied: 'The Queen Mother."

• **Zakhar Dvoiris** masqueraded as a Minister of Public Works in the Soviet Union in the early 1970s and did it so convincingly that he soon had a flat in Moscow, two country houses and an Intourist limousine. He wintered at a luxury hotel on the Black Sea, whooping it up on vodka and caviar and was never, it seems, asked to pay any bills. If you have the right manner it is easier to get away with this sort of thing in rigidly bureaucratic and hierarchical societies. But it is also more dangerous. It is not known what became of him.

• The **Hauptmann von Kopenick** pulled off an astonishing coup in the years before the First World War. He made a close study of Prussian army drill and procedures, dressed up as an officer, took command of a passing platoon of men, marched them on the town of Kopenick and arrested its Mayor, against whom he had a personal grudge. Most of Europe thought this very funny but the Prussians did not.

• **Horace de Vere Cole** was the outstanding English exemplar of this mode. It was he, it's said, who invented the tape trick in which you induce some passer-by on a busy street to hold one end of your measuring tape, pay it out round a corner where you get another stranger to hold the other end, then retire to a vantage-point to see how long they will stand there. He is also said to have led a group of friends to the Strand at rush-hour, cordoned the street off, dug a huge hole in the middle of the road and then quietly gone away.

Expression 2. Keeping a straight face. This is one of the hardest tricks of all.

The 17th century produced one of the all-time greats of the game, perhaps the first man to earn a regular living and considerable fame out of bluff.

He called himself **George Psalmanazar**. It is not known where he got the George from but he took the surname from the name of an Assyrian king in the Old Testament.

A man of many mysteries, largely arising from the fact that he is the sole source of information about his early years, he was, naturally, entirely unreliable. It is not known when he was born – 1679 is the date usually given. Nor is it known where he originated though Gascony is usually credited and it seems to have been somewhere in southern France.

Growing up he showed two promising qualities – a passion for notoriety and a gift for languages. Among leading bluffers all have had the former and a surprisingly high percentage have had the latter.

Some time in his mid teens he went to Germany where he began to build his career, posing as a native of Japan who had been converted to the Christian faith. This made him something of a rarity and there was great public interest. He created his own language, gabbled away in it fluently and devised an alphabet for it, producing 'Japanese' manuscripts. Then he found there was more profit to be had from presenting himself as an unconverted heathen Formosan, observing strange and barbaric devotional rites. He held his own in public disputations with learned Christian divines.

In 1703 Psalmanazar arrived in England and within a few weeks was the sensation of the season. He was taken up by the Bishop of London, who commissioned him to translate the Catechism into 'Formosan'. He dined with the Royal Society, the Earl of Pembroke and other notables, spinning them horrific stories about human sacrifice and cannibalism rampant in his homeland.

'His assurance', someone wrote, 'silenced suspicions of fraud. He made it a practice never to withdraw or modify any statement that he had once made in public.' He was once challenged to prove he was Formosan and his prompt response stands as an object lesson to all aspiring bluffers to this day: 'How can I? If you, sir, were landed on the shores of Formosa and my countrymen said 'Prove to us you are an Englishman', how would you do it? For they would think you suspiciously resembled some of the Dutch traders they had seen but would have no conception of what an Englishman was like.'

There was no answer to that.

Expression 3. The ability to remain calm, however threatening the situation, however inevitable it may seem that your bluff is about to be called.

A good example is **Clifford Irving**, the American novelist, who in the early 1970s succeeded in convincing the New York publishers, McGraw Hill, and *Life* magazine, that he had gained access to the obsessionally reclusive millionaire Howard Hughes and could furnish them with the Hughes memoirs. Scenting enormous sales they gave Irving enormous cheques, totalling nearly one million dollars, the greater part of it payable to 'H. Hughes'. These were paid into a Swiss bank account by Irving's wife who had thoughtfully taken the name of Helga Hughes.

It was a bold, imaginative and carefully executed scheme but Irving's finest moment came when the whole scheme was collapsing about his ears. When reports of the impending book came out Howard Hughes denied any knowledge of Irving or the 'memoirs'. Then the Swiss bank revealed that the cheques had been paid in by a woman. There was further incriminating evidence.

A lesser man would have cut and run at this point but Irving flew to New York, confronted the anxious publishers, answered their questions with a wealth of circumstantial detail, then took the floor.

'There are three possible explanations,' he said. 'First, that I've been dealing all along with an imposter. Second, that Hughes for his own inscrutable purposes used a loyal servant to cash his cheques for him. Third, that I am a hoaxer.' He looked carefully round his rivetted audience, then went on: 'The last of these possibilities I intend to discard. And I hope that you do too.'

They all nodded and several more weeks – and cheques – passed before they realised that they had been fooled once more.

4. Attention to Telling Detail

Bluffer satisfaction is in inverse proportion to the effort involved: the lower the merit, in terms of real knowledge or experience or thought, the better the bluffing has to be to ensure success.

This should not, however, be taken to imply that the good bluffer is entirely ignorant of everything except the techniques of bluffing. It pays to have at least a smattering of genuine knowledge. That is where the Bluffer's Guides are so valuable. And it can sometimes pay handsomely to have a real command of some narrow and esoteric subject. Pooh-Bah, as you will recall, speaks approvingly of 'corroborative detail, intended to give artistic verisimilitude to an otherwise bald and unconvincing narrative.' Many master bluffers have recognised the importance of this.

Example 1. Maundy Gregory (who made a fortune after World War I by selling political honours), when he was looking for a house in central London, had one vital requirement – it should be number 10 of whatever street. This was to make sure the secretaries in his Whitehall office would interrupt him from time to time with the words 'Number Ten on the 'phone, sir' which vastly impressed visitors.

Example 2. 'The Man who Never Was', was the brainchild of a naval intelligence officer called Ewen

Montagu who went to astonishing lengths to make the bluff convincing. The aim was to deceive the Germans about the impending invasion of Sicily, to give them the impression that the actual allied targets were Sardinia, Corsica and Greece. This was achieved by having the body of a British Staff officer, carrying spoof letters to the allied commanders in North Africa, washed ashore on a part of the Spanish coast where it was known the local German agent was in close cahoots with the Spanish authorities.

It was all very thoroughly and delicately done and it worked so well that two weeks after the allied forces had landed in Sicily the Germans were still holding back, believing that the main blow was yet to fall in Greece.

Example 3. An R.A.F. sergeant used his mastery of the service's forms and procedures to post himself to a non-existent airfield in a remote corner of East Anglia. He took crates of assorted forms with him and before long had built up, entirely on paper but all quite correct there, a sizeable station. He drew pay for all the staff. He was only rumbled after many months when some Air Vice Marshal, motoring nearby, decided to pay an unscheduled visit.

The Master

Wilson Mizner (for it is he) was born in California in 1876 and from the start he had a lot going for him. His family were the big-shots of their hometown, Benicia. His father was a successful politician and all-round speculator, sometime envoy in Guatemala where Wilson picked up fluent Spanish (which came in handy as Latin when he started his working life as a salesman with Dr. Silas Slocum's travelling medicine show). Mother was a formidable and formative influence. When Wilson, as a young man, wired home for money, she wired back: 'I didn't get your telegram.'

And there was an elder brother, Addison, who became a multi-millionaire in the 1920s, building 'dream palaces' in Florida for the very wealthy. Addison developed a number of profitable sidelines, including a factory for 'antique' furniture. His workers were trained to fire air-gun pellets into the woodwork and Addison would walk down the production line crying: 'Shoot from the side boys. A worm always charges at a piece of furniture from an angle.'

This was the great flowering period for the all American conman and Wilson Mizner was the flower of them all. His genius was for conversation. He could keep people laughing for hours on end, while he was robbing them blind. He called it 'gentle larceny'. He liked people – particularly his own kind and easy-going women – but had no respect for anyone or any institution. He was rough and sleazy in manner and shockingly outspoken. Damon Runyon said he was 'the greatest man-about-town any town ever had.'

Wilson tried his hand at every line of business that offered high profits for the least possible effort. He was by turns, and often simultaneously, gambler and cardsharp, fairground barker, art dealer, prize-fighter and promoter of fights and manager of would-be champions, saloon bar singer, song-writer, successful Broadway playwright (he just talked – he had a partner to write it down), screenwriter in the early days of Hollywood, salesman, company promoter, estate agent, hotelier, socialite and seducer.

He learned his trade in Dawson City during the Yukon gold rush from such experts as 'Soapy' Smith and 'Swiftwater Bill'. One of their rackets was the 'badger game'. The victim, just back from a hard stint of mining, would be lured into a young woman's apartment. Fifteen minutes later Mizner, in the role of outraged husband, would crash through the door waving a six-shooter and collect hefty 'damages'.

Most nights he spent gambling, usually poker. He would bet on anything, so long as the odds were right, and go to extraordinary lengths to win. One afternoon in Atlantic City he was sitting in the sun with a gang of like-minded 'sporting men' when one of them spotted a gigantic pair of feet sticking out of the first floor window of the hotel opposite. They began to guess at the height of the owner of such prodigious feet, backing their estimates with money. Mizner let the others commit themselves, then made the lowest guess. When the man with the feet stood up he was seen to be a dwarf. Mizner had come across him in New York, realised his potential, paid his fare down and set the whole thing up.

He had the four key qualities in greater abundance, perhaps, than anyone who has ever lived. When a reporter asked for the secret of his success he replied in one word: 'Impudence'.

In the very end he was buoyant and unrepentant. Coming out of a long coma on his death bed he was shocked to find a priest at the bedside: 'Why should I talk to you?' he said. 'I've just been talking to your boss.'

THE BLUFFER'S BASIC LIBRARY

Accountancy – 'Adds up a to an imaginative total.'
Exchange and Mart

British Class – 'Admirably lowers one's sights.'   *County Life*

Computers – 'A calculated triumph.' *Screen Watcher's Weekly*

Golf – 'Really swinging.'   *Carnoustie Herald*

Literature – 'Eminently readable.'   *Musical Opinion*

Management – 'A well-controlled text.'   *Business First*

Marketing – 'A good buy to all that.'   *What?*

Philosophy – 'A book to set you thinking.'   *Daily Wail*

Photography – 'Really clicks! '   *Organists' Bulletin*

Publishing – 'A book for the damned.' *Bookseller's Almanac*

Sex – 'There should be an enormous demand for it.'
Woman's Fortnightly

Theatre – 'Had them rolling in the Isles.'   *Orkney Gazette*

Wine – 'You will be amazed at its presumption.'
The Imbiber

Champagne – 'A frothy concoction.'   *Wine, Women & Song*

Archaeology – 'Dig this.'   *Cairo Express*

Weather Forecasting – 'An unpredictable delight.'
News of the World

Racing – 'A sure winner.'   *Fur & Feather*

Astrology – 'Unforeseen pleasure.'   *Radio Times*

THE AUTHOR

Peter Gammond first showed signs of becoming one of the world's leading bluffers when he was about six months old and managed to convince his parents that he was growing up to be a pleasant and normal child. But by the age of three they had begun to realise that there was something distinctly odd about him. At school he came into his own, bluffing his way through the requisite exams without actually bothering to learn anything.

He managed to avoid all the famous battles of World War II and returned to Oxford University where he obtained first-class honours in bar billiards and free-verse. He then joined a famous record company as their leading musical expert (which he considers to be one of his major bluffing achievements) and only just failed by twenty people or so to become managing director.

Almost imperceptibly becoming a freelance writer, he spent many years as a record reviewer, saving time by listening to LPs on 78 rpm equipment. In 1964 he wrote *Bluff Your Way in Music* and has had very little work from the musical establishment ever since. This was updated and re-issued in 1985 and was followed by Bluffer's Guides to Golf, Class, Opera and Jazz. He also has a passing interest in literature and a consuming interest in real ale. Meanwhile he lives up to his family motto:

Dum spiro bluffo.